LINES FOR ALL OCCASIONS

Tweets & Status Updates

KNOCK KNOCK®
VENICE, CALIFORNIA

Created and published by Knock Knock
Distributed by Who's There Inc.
Venice, CA 90291
knockknockstuff.com

This book is a work of humor meant solely for
entertainment purposes. Actually utilizing the
lines contained herein may be illegal or lead to
bodily injury. The publisher and anyone associated
with the production of this book do not advocate
breaking the law. In no event will Knock Knock be
liable to any reader for any damages, including
direct, indirect, incidental, special, consequential,
or punitive arising out of or in connection with the
use of the lines contained in this book. So there.

ISBN: 978-160106308-3
UPC: 825703-50114-8

10 9 8 7 6 5 4

Contents

*@**Hipster** Oh my God.*
People are actually dancing. #WTF

Introduction

PREPARING TO POST WITH APLOMB

The tide of social media has turned. No longer merely ubiquitous, the World Wide Web has become a tsunami of status updates, Tweets, and sound bites all in the name of staying connected—or getting noticed. With more than half a billion Facebook users as of 2010, learning how to skillfully surf the Internet—and more importantly how to stand out—is a downright necessity.

In order to attract attention in a sea of overshares, however, you'll need to polish your posts to a perfect shine to garner maximum exposure. As the actor and Tweeter extraordinaire Ashton Kutcher observed, "we're at a place now with social media where a single person's voice can be as powerful as an entire news network—that is the power of the social web."

Whether you're a social media novice or an online guru, thinking up things to post can be perplexing, and despite what the so-called experts say there isn't one foolproof strategy to increase your friend or followers list—other than being witty, that is. By picking up *Tweets and Status Updates for All Occasions* you're not only well on your way to getting peoples' attention, but keeping it, too (no small feat on the Internet). The lines herein provide guidance for every possible circumstance worth posting about, from the daily grind to the weather to divorce, and furnish you with plenty of famous examples featuring celebrities both real and imagined for inspiration. Perusing these pages virtually guarantees you'll be a featured Top Tweeter in no time.

For such a relatively new phenomenon, just how important is it to be a savvy social media user? In short—very. Your potential audience is staggering; close to two billion people worldwide use the Internet. According to Facebook, 50 percent of its users access the site on any given day. What's more, a mind-boggling total of 700 billion minutes are spent clicking, tagging, and waxing mundane on the site per month. The microblogging site Twitter is also making an impact; the site already has over 165 million users as of 2010 and adds about 300,000 more every day. And its output is impressive as well; the site's users post upwards of 65 million Tweets *every day*.

Social media isn't just good for your ego, either; according to an article published in *Psychology Today* the sites can have a generally positive effect on your real social life. That is, of course, if you avoid the dreaded embarrassment of being unfriended. The best way to ensure a rapt audience is to keep your posts current, and thereby provide a vicarious peek into your (surely) fascinating life. Today's mobile devices provide users nearly unlimited access to the Internet, and with it, unlimited opportunities to keep friends and followers abreast.

Tweets and Status Updates for All Occasions is your guidebook to guaranteeing all your posts inspire comments, elicit reposts and retweets, and exponentially build your friend and fan bases. Organized by theme and carefully edited to provoke the appropriate response—be it laughter, sympathy, or envy— the chapters herein enable you to both transcend and lampoon topics of universal interest.

The beauty of cultivating a dedi- cated online following is that you can avoid pesky face-to-face inter- action entirely. If words fail you, there is no awkward silence to con- tend with—simply pull out your copy of *Tweets and Status Updates for All Occasions*, choose an appropriate entry, and bask in the warm glow of the computer laughing out loud.

OFFICE UPDATES

When it's just business

No matter their position in the corporate food chain, office workers across the board share one powerful bond: killing time on the Internet. With the advent of social media, employees now have numerous platforms from which to distract themselves, vent, and generally dissect the professional world between the hours of nine and five. Whether your intention

11

Big Brother

What you post stays put—and is more public than you may think. A survey conducted by CareerBuilder.com found that up to 45 percent of employers used information uncovered online, including Facebook profiles, to evaluate job candidates. Unfortunately, deleting that drunken picture isn't always a sure thing. Facebook has come under scrutiny for keeping deleted photos online and accessible for up to two and a half years.

is to advance your career or simply comment on the higher-ups' incompetence, conveying it with the appropriate brevity is of paramount importance.

Keeping up with what's happening online is itself a type of work, but there are even benefits to the *actual* work you do. According to a report from the University of Melbourne, employees who browsed the Internet between office tasks were up to 9 percent *more* productive than their coworkers who did not.

Once you've carved out some time for yourself on the clock, the question becomes what to post. No matter your station there are surely innumerable others in the same position, making it all but impossible *not* to inspire a devoted following that can relate to the witty quips found in this chapter. If you're complaining or gloating, someone out there is too—while procrastinating online. Remember, it doesn't matter whether they like your post because they can relate or respond simply out of schadenfreude, as long as it promotes your feed.

Intern

@Intern First day in the real world! #madphotocopyskills

———•———

@Intern Second day in the real world. Is it possible to get your foot stuck in the door? #interningsucks

———•———

@NewKid They do say you have to get your hands dirty to get anywhere in this world. #cleaningofficebathroom

———•———

@Neophyte Need the experience but hate the early mornings. #internalconflict

———•———

@Trainee Bulk staples and sticky notes—real cheap. #extraincome

———•———

@Intern Summer is overrated. #rationalizing

@Neophyte Cutting your teeth
is a pain. #nodentalplan

@Rookie Already tackling some
important paperwork. #unemployment

@Trainee What a great internship!
So sad to leave. #willworkforbeer

@Intern The name's John. RT
@HeadHoncho Been great having
you on board this summer!
#bonvoyagepaul

Receptionist

@FrontDesk Good morning
everyone! Looking forward to
the day! #increasedmydosage

@YesMaam Please hold. #forever
#limbo #goodluck!

@Secretary Calling in sick today. #noanswer

@Reception I'm putting more than callers on hold. #mylife

@YesMaam You have a nice day, too. #asshole

@FrontDesk A receptionist's work is never done. #oncall

@Secretary What does this company do exactly? #disconnected

@YesMaam Would you like to be put on hold or try back later? #itscalledemail

---

@Reception Sooo weird. Calls for the assistant job keep getting dropped. #howtogetahead

@**Secretary** Thanks job market.

Assistant

@**RightHand** Should be thankful
I even have a job! #glassceiling

@**Subordinate** Babysitting
does prepare you for the real
world. #executiveassistance

Tweet Job

Celebrities need cash to support their lavish
lifestyles, and some have figured out a way
to increase their cash flow by simply lifting a
finger—literally. New advertising services connect companies with cash-hungry "stars" who
will send sponsored Tweets for a fee. Public
figures such as Lindsay Lohan and Khloe Kar-
dashian can command prices of nearly $3,000
per Tweet. Fame is expensive, after all.

@PersonalAssistant Picking up
dry cleaning on my lunch
break. #starving

———•·•———

@BigCheese But not offline.
#bigbrother RT **@Admin**
@BigCheese is out of the office!

———•·•———

@Subordinate Adding spoon-feeding
to my resume. #assistedliving

———•·•———

@Gofer Lips chapped. #asskissing

———•·•———

@PersonalAssistant Morning
coffee run = $4 + 20 minutes
outside the office. #fairtrade

———•·•———

@Admin Think I just fell off the
corporate ladder. #lawsuit

———•·•———

@PersonalAssistant Trying to sleep
my way to the top. #oversleptagain

Head Honcho

@CornerOffice It's lonely at the top. #ishouldbuysomefriends

@Kingpin Loving this escargot! #expenseeverything

@TheMan And on the fifth day I created an offshore bank account. #godcomplex

@BigCheese Weird. Everyone looks like ants! #viewfromthetop

@TheMan Just beat solitaire. Again. #smartestguyintheroom

@CornerOffice It's hard to put a figure on success. I've never been very good with numbers. #top1percent

Short and Tweet

With its elegant emphasis on brevity, online chatting has elevated acronyms to new creative heights:

- AAK: Asleep at keyboard
- ?^: Want to hook up?
- 2BZ4UQT: Too busy for you, cutie
- LOL: Laughing out loud
- ROTFL: Rolling on the floor laughing (see LOL)
- GBTW: Get back to work

@BigCheese LOL! RT **@BiggerCheese** Profit sharing = posting my bank statement to the company blog. #officehumor

---

@TheMan No man is an island. #iownanisland

@Kingpin Bored, directionless. #weekend

IT Support

@Techie Just hit restart.
#stopbuggingme

@BigBrother I can tell when you're
looking at porn. #blackmail

@EyeTee Hitting it always
works. #suits

@Techie I think u have the wrong
feed. #crossedwires RT **@Girl**
Thanks for the good time last night.

@Hi-Tech Just checking out some
websites. Might read some
blogs. #work

@Techie Finding it hard to
concentrate. So many
distractions! #readingabook

@Hi-Tech Not sure if it's my job or the coffee. #wired

------•------

@BigBrother Delete. #keytomysuccess

Creative Team

@Designer Rendering myself obsolete. #softwaredesign

------•------

@Editor Keep it short and sweet. #tweet

------•------

@Illustrator Seeking nude models for private in-home sessions. #sketchy

------•------

@Editor Polishing up a piece of creative nonfiction. #resume

------•------

@Designer Doing a lot of pro bono work these days. #mybandflyers

@Creative Just finished a great spec script about a new website that wastes everyone's time. #imitatinglife

---

@Illustrator Trying to come up with something original. #drawingablank

---

@Designer Taking my laptop up to the roof. #layout

@1000Monkeys Just finished Macbeth. #next

Sales and Marketing

@SocialMediaMarketer Giving a lecture 2nite on #whytwittersux. Hope 2 see you there!

@SnakeOil You don't need these. They won't make you prettier or happier. #honesty

@Salesman I ♥ people w/ money! #targetmarket

@MarketingMatters Sure, there are things I should work on. #commission

---

@Salesman Super excited to be building my own brand! #pyramidscheme

---

@MarketingMatters Sounds terrible. #freemarket

@Salesman I've got something to say. #powerpoint

@SnakeOil This Tweet, a steal at $10! #2good2refuse

@MarketingMatters This job makes me so dizzy. #spin

@Telemarketer Back 2 work! #dinnertime

@SocialMediaMarketer SEO. SEM. #SOB

@WillyLoman Besides other sales peeps, does anyone read these? #existentialcrisis

No Pain, No Gain

Office work gets a bad rap as a "safe" career route, but it turns out that all that Internet surfing can actually be dangerous. The Occupational Safety and Health Administration warns that musculoskeletal disorders (MSDs) can result from awkward positions and repetitive tasks. They recommend incorporating ergonomic practices, such as comfortable working postures, into your workday—and leaving your desk once in a while.

DAILY
DOCUMENTATION

When everything matters

THE DIGITAL ERA HAS PROVIDED us with a never-ending forum to share even the most mundane of details—and share we do. In order to maintain the interest of our vast but capricious audience, however, it's important to ensure that our observations, complaints, and quips are actually amusing. In this over-saturated environment, the only way to rise above the din of digital

Tip: Look Here

Your profile picture says a lot more about you than what you look like. Vet the message you send by considering what many bloggers concur is the most befitting. Close-ups appear to be cries for attention, whereas shots taken from a distance infer a lack of openness. The group shot implies that you need too much external validation, and party shots, of course, just make you look drunk. Just right? A sober snapshot from an appropriate distance.

information is make sure your ordinary updates are anything but.

For the most part, however, life isn't terribly exciting. Momentous occasions like weddings and birthdays, not to mention devastating events like natural disasters, are hard to come by. Fortunately, almost everyone has some raw material—something to talk about.

According to the US Department of Labor, most of us spend between five and six hours a day participating in leisure activities, including everything from exercising to watching television to socializing (the face-to-face kind). Surely, you can find something to say about all manner of daily events—you just need total confidence in how fascinating your life really is.

The lines in this chapter span the situations and locations you are most likely to encounter on a regular day. Stuck in line? Going hard at the gym? Waiting for a movie to start? Keep your audience in the know. From acerbic observations to straight-up bitchiness, ensure your observations and complaints are at least slightly inflammatory to help distinguish you from the mundane masses.

On Vacation

@BonVivant Whoops! Seem to have lost my passport! #permanentvacation

---

@BackPacker We're being introduced to so many new foods! #cockroaches

---

@Tourist Looking at the Eiffel Tower. #meh

@FannyPacker This place rules! All the food I ♥ + my actual bedroom! #staycation

---

@BonVivant Luckily, this isn't my first time summering in France. #egotrip

---

@BackPacker Have stopped giving locals the thumbs up. #badsign

@Tourist Gift shopping today. Hope to bring a little piece of NY home with us! #bedbugs

Shopping

@GroceryShopper Why don't we just club baby seals while we're at it? #plasticplease

---

@Clientele Headed back for more. #returns

@Shopper Does insurance cover retail therapy? #justchecking

@Customer Turns out, you can't buy love. #butyoucouldtry

@Clientele Checking out. Cashier's giving me a mean look. Now telling me to quit Tweeting. Now walking away. #hopeless

@**Shopper** Library card was
declined :(#badcredit

—•—

@**Clientele** Snoozing in
housewares. #checkedout

Online

@**NewUser** I just won the
Nigerian lottery! #haters

—•—

@**Tweeter** Updating. #update

—•—

@**LittleBird** Tweet Tweet,
bang bang. #failwhale

—•—

@**FBFriend** Does this profile
picture make me look fat?
#askanhonestquestion

—•—

@**Tweeter** Just hit my 500th
follower! #strangelyhollow

@Blogger Looking for the best way
to mail my rent check. #post

* * *

@FBUser I think my
laptop is gaining weight.
#stoppedrunning

* * *

@Tweeter Writing this now.
Might write something else
in a few minutes. #tweet

Bad Boys?

When the Manchester, England, police
announced their plan to Tweet about every
incident for a full twenty-four hours in 2010,
many anticipated a glimpse of real-life drama.
Situations of note, however, were limited to
a woman missing her bus and a trash can on
the highway. A word cloud generated from
the more than three thousand Tweets didn't
provide much more excitement, featuring
standouts such as "man," "abandoned," "car."

Gym

@Flex I'm like a burned CD! #ripped

@Dumbbell Can you work
out how to get out of working
out? #mundanephilosophy

@MuscleHead Size does
matter. #awkwardsilence

@GymRat Hitting the
showers. #angerissues

@Dumbbell Working some
things out. #armschestlegs

@GymRat Today, I'm letting my laptop
do the work. #runningaprogram

@MuscleHead Am I cut or
what? #bleedinghelp

@Flex Argh! Fingers cramping!
#forgot2stretch

Dining

@Foodie I promised myself
I would never Tweet while
eating. #eatingmywords

@Boozehound What time
is it? #noonsomewhere

@LunchBreak Just finished Tweeting
updates. Strangely, I don't feel that
hungry anymore. #twitterfeed

@Gourmand Posting pictures from
last night's invite-only dinner.
#partyfoul

@Foodie I only read Tweets sent from
no more than five miles away.
#locavore

Tweet Like It's Your Job

Social media can often feel like a popularity contest from another world—because it is. Luckily social media scientist Dan Zarrella has codified that elusive marker of popularity on the World Wide Web: the retweet. Aside from being popular in the first place, tactics can seem counterintuitive. He advises appealing directly to followers to retweet, as well as yawn-inducing strategies such as being an early bird and Tweeting about . . . Twitter.

@**Gourmand** Stuffing myself with foie gras topped by quail eggs and truffle oil! #eatme

———·•·———

@**LostAppetite** Forget— what's it called when a mama bird coughs up a boring, already digested worm to feed her needy young? #retweet

Waiting Around

@BankPatron Been standing in line for an hour. What's the point, anyway? #withdrawn

@FrequentFlyer At airport security. This is kind of sexy . . . #fullbodyscan

@FrequentFlyer This is even sexier. #optedout

@InTraffic Is this safe?

@BankPatron Guy in front of me is holding everyone up. #skimask

@Juror The courthouse is very theatrical today. #waitingforgodot

@**Nerd** It's 6 am. Standing in a line, outside, in the cold, to get a new iPhone. #sentfrommyiphone

Doctor's Office

@**Patient** Anyone want to cosponsor my copay? #groupplan

@**Doctor** When you think about it, we're all dying. #bitterpill

---

@**HeadCase** My symptoms have all the signs of an aggressive marketing campaign. #viral

---

@**Patient** Bored. Think I'll try to download some iMagazines to read. #highlights1992

@**Doctor** An interesting case. I need to consult with a colleague. #google

@HeadCase The insurance company is disputing my claim. #selfmedication

***

@Doctor Bend over. #cough

Bar

@Drunk If I don't update in the next hour, check the bathroom floor. #tequila

***

@Hungover This morning I wish I wore my sunglasses—last night. #walkofshame

***

@Bartender The more you drink, the less attractive you become. #tip

***

@Drunk 2 much 2 drink. Taking off my shoes. #girlsgonemild

***

@Hungover It was the beer Tweeting last night. #excuses

@Sober There's a bitter taste in this vodka that I can't place. #remorse

At the Movies

@MovieCritic This Tweet totally sucks. #spoileralert

@Cinephile Don't get it. Loving it! #arthouse

@BackRow Can't hear you because of some awful hissing noise. #sssssssssshhhhhhhhhh

---

@MovieCritic The film depicts a sad figure who is obsessed with life's banal details. #biopic

---

@Cinephile Neck hurts. #frontrowblues

@BackRow @Cinephile Theater
is a wreck, screen is too small,
but the popcorn is free. Neck's
great, too. #streaming

Concert

@Rocker Da da dadada da
dadadadadadada da dada dadada
da da daa daa dadadada
da da. #airguitar

TwitSpeak

Social media is nothing if not self-referential,
and the growing lexicon of the Twitterverse is
no exception. Consider these TwitterTerms:

- Twillionaire: user with over a million
  followers
- Twilebrities: people who are famous as a
  result of Tweeting
- Twitition: a Twitter-distributed petition
- Twitticide: a person who deletes his or her
  Twitter account

@MusicLover Yes! Totally recognize this song! #myringtone

@Rocker My memory of last night's show is hazy. #fogmachine

@Hipster Oh my God. People are actually dancing. #WTF

@MusicLover It's sad when a musical genre loses popularity. #theblues

---

@Rocker The dressing room has great acoustics. #stagefright

Weather

@WindyCity Everyone says the wind does wonders for my hair. #blowinghotair

@**Indoors** Internet says it's
sunny outside. #FML

———•◆•———

@**WeatherMan** Got those rainy-
day-so-might-as-well-download-
pirated-movies blues. #torrential

———•◆•———

@**WeatherReport** Ow!
Ouch! #whatthehail

———•◆•———

@**HeatWave** Downloaded
too much sun. #burned

———•◆•———

@**WeatherMan** So over this
chilly weather. #toocool

———•◆•———

@**HeatWave** This weather makes
me horny. #hotandsticky

———•◆•———

@**Dorothy** So hard to type! Will
update when I figure out where
we are. #overtherainbow

INTERPERSONAL POSTS

When you care enough to chat

WHATEVER THE RELATIONSHIP—
from the spouse you see every
day to the second cousin you
haven't spoken to since the family
reunion—social media has, for
better or worse, brought us closer
together and forced us to interact
more frequently. So while distance
may make the heart grow fonder,
frankly, the kind of distance we're
used to is no longer an option.

Our Man in Nigeria

Spammers have long been dashing hopes of would-be Nigerian lottery winners and anyone seeking cheap erectile dysfunction pills. Having successfully made the move to social networks, it's now been reported that nearly 24 percent of Tweets are actually generated by bots or automated programs. When sorting through your status updates, look out for common words found in spam: shipping!, today!, here!, available!, fingertips!, and online!

When it comes to family, you may be tempted to take the safe route and avoid friending or following close family members altogether. But you're going to have to step on a lot of (related) toes to get away with that particular maneuver. Once invited, however, relatives are there to stay. Why not mine the many opportunities for comic relief and keep your friends informed of all the embarrassing bits before they get to it first? In this chapter you'll find plenty of inspiration and lines to quote verbatim while commenting on that universally relatable topic—the dysfunctional family.

Romantic relationships are also easily complicated by online forums. Perhaps you're looking to find someone special (or simply adequate) on a dating site, or want to inform your extended network that it didn't work out. Either way, tracking your every romantic move is essential to avoid appearing like a loveless loser. Presentation is key. With so much on the line (your very chances of reproductive success), it's of the utmost importance that you articulate what makes you so special, or in the case of those already committed—right.

Parents

@**ProudParent** Baby just
sent her first Tweet!

———•·•———

@**Baby** ffffffffffffffffffffff

———•·•———

@**ConcernedParents** Where do our
kids pick this language up? #retweet

———•·•———

@**HeadoftheFamily** There are so
many things that I want to pass
down to my children. #filesharing

———•·•———

@**Mom** Uploading pix from
the honeymoon. #TMI

———•·•———

@**Dad** It's ten o'clock and I know
where my kids are. #GPS

———•·•———

@**HeadoftheFamily** Some animals are
known to eat their young. #goodnight

@**Mom** Unfortunately you can't choose
your family. #thankgod4antidepressants

———•·•———

@**Dad** Playing catch with
my son. #bonk

———•·•———

@**Mom** Loving everything my
daughter's loving! #parenttrap

———•·•———

@**Procreator** Anything for a
free phone. #familyplan

Kids

@**Sister** R 2. RT @**Brother**
R Not. #siblingrivalry

———•·•———

@**Brother** First update in two months.
Anyone notice? #middlechild

———•·•———

@**Sibling** Don't even try to read
my diary. #passwordprotected

@**Son** Tweet! #cryforattention

@**Twin1** th my brother. RT
@**Twin2** Hanging wi

@**Sister** Has anyone seen my
brother's blankie? #cruel

@**Daughter** Finally figured it
out. So simple! #adopted

@**Teen** OMG! I H8 EVRY1!
#puberty

@**Sister** @**OtherSister** Finding that we
have a lot in common. #mutualdislike

@**Son** Leaving school.
Heading home. #prodigal

@**Sibling** Even my Twitter account is a
hand-me-down. #everythingisrelative

@Son Working on my history homework. Terrified. #greekmyths

@Daughter My mom just tried to friend me on Facebook. #ignore

Extended Family

@Granddad In my day, we would have to type in 2 feet of snow. #uphill

Tip: Frenemies

Social networking sites are incredible for reconnecting with old friends and meeting new ones. But take heed—not everyone you encounter online is really your friend. People to avoid include parents (unconditional love is actually a myth), ex-lovers (stalking is not actually cute), strangers (not actually human), and, of course, bosses (feigning sickness while simultaneously posting pictures from the beach is not actually multitasking).

@**Daughter** At @**Mom**'s third wedding, first civil union. #modernfamily

———•—•———

@**Cousin** Neither do mine. RT @**Brother** My pants don't fit anymore. #badjeans

———•—•———

@**Cousin** Trying to connect with @**SecondCousin**. #norelation

———•—•———

@**Nephew** Had a great interview with @**UncleDave**! Fingers crossed for a callback. #nepotism

———•—•———

@**Granddad** Nice pictures. Hawaii must be beautiful at Xmas. #guilttrip

———•—•———

@**Aunt** Saw ur latest profile pic—diet is really working! #nofilter

———•—•———

@**Grandmom** Looking forward to seeing everyone at my birthday. #willpower

@Granddad Hiding the family jewels. #deeplydisturbing

———•———

@UrCousin Watching the big fight. Got money on your **@Mom**. #familyfeud

Marriage

@Girlfriend Totes. RT **@Boyfriend** Hey **@Girlfriend**, want 2 hang 4eva? #indecentproposal

———•———

@Fiancée Give me another ring later. #diamond

———•———

@Husband My wife is an animal in bed! #sloth

———•———

@Wife Working on keeping our relationship private. #oops

Searching for Love

If you're looking for love, maybe it's time to log on. No longer hiding behind a computer screen, online dating has shed any stigma it once had and has gone public. In the United States alone, it's a $1 billion a year industry. There are drawbacks, of course, to meeting potential dates in virtual reality rather than face-to-face, however. Experts warn that online daters tend to inflate their salary by 20 percent and their height by two inches.

@SnuggleBear Anyone know how to change my screen name? #wifesetupaccount

@Wife Not all change is good. #keepingmyname

@Husband We need to Tweet with each other more. #couplestherapy

@**Wife** @**Husband**'s on a
business trip. #bzzzzzzz

———•·•———

@**Husband** Running out of
things to talk about. #

———•·•———

@**Wife** I ♥ my husband.
#ijustdontlikehim

———•·•———

@**Husband** So happy! What
could ruin this? #kids

———•·•———

@**Wife** Marriage is overrated.
#divorce

Singlehood

@**FreeBird** I'm loving being
single! #cryingontheinside

———•·•———

@**Single** Am I looking for love in all
the wrong places? #facebookstalk

@Solo I'm in love! #newflatscreenTV

@BitterPill My ex looks super puffy in his profile picture! #schadenfreude

---

@FreeBird My side of the bed = the whole bed. #brightside

@Single Can't wait until Saturday. #datewithmom #unconditionallove #freedinner

---

@Solo At home researching places to meet people. The Internet says to meet people on the Internet. #fail

---

@BitterPill Date is looking annoyed. Don't see what the problem is. #blind

---

@Solo I am such a player! #onlinegames

@BitterPill Looking out for number one. #loneliestnumber

@FreeBird FTR I really miss building up another person's ego. #jk

@Solo I've got a great personality. And a sad one. And an angry one. #aboutme

@Single Technically, I'm not alone. #cats

@FreeBird Dancing in my underwear!

Friendship

@Buddy What R friends 4? #rhetoricaltweet

@Frenemy H8 U! JK! #orami?

@**Friend** The airplane noises
are a big turnoff. #wingman

@**iPal** I've lost so many
friends. #deletedaccount

@**Buddy** Just friended myself. #meta

@**Frenemy** Hanging with you.
#totallybored

@**Friend** What are friends
for? #airportrides

@**iPal** Friends don't let friends
unfriend friends. #intervention

@**Buddy** Thank god for
buds! #happyhour

@**Friend** Cute pix! #untag

@**Frenemy** Wouldn't it be cool if
we were actually related?
#datingyourmom

———•—•———

@**iPal** It's so good to reconnect with
you! #secondaryembarrassment

———•—•———

@**Frenemy** I really like your new
boyfriend @**Naive**! #newcrush

Sex in Public

Gadgets are increasingly prevalent in every
area of our lives—including our sex lives.
According to a survey conducted by the tech
website Retrevo.com, about 36 percent of
the under thirty-five set either text, Tweet, or
check Facebook post coitus, and about one in
ten of those younger than twenty-five don't
mind electronic interruptions (and not of the
fun, vibrating, battery-operated sort) during
the act itself.

CULTURAL
COMMENTS

When it's history in the making

THROUGHOUT THE AGES WE HAVE
looked to public figures—politicians, actors, artists, famous people
of no discernible talent whatso-
ever—to help us understand our
existence, from the big questions to
the latest fashions to how much we
should weigh. No longer, however,
must we wade arduously through
the pages of books or magazines
to find out what the famous are

Olde Tyme Tweets

While the truncated tech-speak of acronyms is a favorite critique of technology, it's not as newfangled a concept as it seems. It wasn't long after the debut of the telegraph in the nineteenth century that books offering code words became available. Because telegraph operators often charged extra for messages over a certain length, it was cheaper to communicate via handy abbreviations such as RUSSET ("bank just robbed").

thinking—now we only need an Internet connection.

But what about those past public figures who didn't have the world at their fingertips—wouldn't they have had plenty to add to the pop culture conversation? We may never know how social media would have shaped previous historical events and movements, be they artistic,

religious, or just plain historic—
but we can sure speculate.

Of course, the idea of putting
words into the screens of deceased
public figures is nothing new.
Plenty of people have started feeds
and pages in homage. Just because
it's been done before doesn't mean
you can't do it, and do a better job,
to boot, however. After all, where
would Andy Warhol (featured
in this very chapter) be without
his source material? The fact of
the matter is that the world has
changed a lot—and very rapidly—
since the invention of the Internet.
Thanks to Al Gore's ingenuity, we
now have ever-expanding access to
innumerable new ideas, all ripe for
riffing and improving upon—as
well as the insight that only hind-
sight can provide.

Musicians

@ElvisPresley Nothing much happening in the building. Might leave soon.

———

@KarenCarpenter It's Monday and it's raining. #bummedout

———

@KurtCobain @C's being a total bitch. #aboutagirl

———

@BobMarley Attn: spring breakers— jammin' **@RebelSmokehouse** tonight! #hopeulikejammin2

———

@JohnLennon Chilling in bed. Naked. With my wife. #imagine

———

@RobertJohnson Supposed to meet someone tonight but could go either way. #crossroads

@BillieHoliday @MilesDavis 2 wet to meet up 2day. #stormyweather

---

@MilesDavis It's raining outside. Unmotivated. Ugh. Why even bother anymore? Do my friends even like me? #kindofblue

---

@JerryGarcia No one takes me seriously. #dancingbears

@LouisArmstrong Working up a sweat! #jazzercise

@MichaelJackson Lost my glove. Retracing my steps. #moonwalk

@JohnnyCash Deciding what to wear tonight. #black

@JimiHendrix I've been Tweeting for years. #experienced

@WolfgangAmadeusMozart My server just died, guess I'll have to get back to the studio. #requiem

———•———

@JimMorrison I give and I give and I give of myself onstage—I am constantly exposing myself! #lizardking

Leading Men and Women

@MarilynMonroe Met @JackieO for the first time tonight, she had a nice hat. #overrated

———•———

@CharlieChaplin Awkward silence. #trycircusmusic

———•———

@JohnWayne Studying for my next role. Got a job on a real ranch—stoked! #brokebackmountain

———•———

@RonaldReagan So L8. Hitting the sack. #bedtime4bonzo

@**BruceLee** Did u know I can kill with a single keystroke? #clickenterthedragon.com

———•••———

@**GrouchoMarx** Terrible dinner—not even sure what we ate. #ducksoup

———•••———

@**PaulNewman** R these eggs organic? #myown

More Than Words

In 2010 Stephen Fry, the British writer and actor who boasts a Twitter following of around 1.5 million, set about to select the world's "most beautiful Tweet" for a Welsh literary festival. The winning Tweet was composed by Canada's Marc MacKenzie under the screen name @marcmack, who posted: "I believe we can build a better world! Of course, it'll take a whole lot of rock, water & dirt. Also, not sure where to put it."

@MarlonBrando I'm more of a fun-loving uncle. #godfather

———•———

@AlfredHitchcock Staring into the sky, aimlessly. #birds

———•———

@OrsonWelles Where do you do your thinking? I always find inspiration in my garden. #rosebud

———•———

@JoanCrawford Having the kids over for dinner. What should I have the chef prepare? #mommiedearest

———•———

@Lassie **@SonofLassie** It's nearly 3 am! #comehome

———•———

@LucilleBall Does anyone know where the hell Desi is? #nothome

———•———

@HowardHughes Achoo! #weareallgoingtodie

Authors

@WilliamShakespeare OMG! I've got it—2B or not 2B? #thatISthequestion

@JaneAusten Writer's block's a bitch and my maid is really slacking—hate Mondays! #prideandprejudice

@JDSalinger Mr. Salinger requests that you cease and desist from following this feed immediately. #don'tgoogleme

@JRRTolkien Nope. My old lady's being a complete ORK! RT **@Gandalf** D&D 2nite, dudes? #middleearth

@eecummings CAN' t waitfor thEnExt SEA son. #madmen

@WilliamFaulkner Can't turn my ringer off! Frustrating! #thesoundandthefury

Netiquette

To avoid the mortifying shame of being un-friended or unfollowed, keep the self-indulgent posting to a minimum and steer clear of certain faux pas. Posts to avoid include one-word transmissions, because "sad" or "frustrating" are just that; drunken rants that only communicate that you are, in fact, drunk; using all caps; and live updates of sporting events, television shows, or worse yet, mundane details like what you're eating for dinner.

@ErnestHemingway
Strawberry daiquiri = my idea.
#ohyeahandiwritebooks2

@PhilipKDick Told u so.

@GeorgeEliot LOL! RT
@Maxim Dear **@GeorgeEliot**,
U R eligible for 20% off our
newsstand price! #boyswillbegirls

@EdgarAllanPoe Wuz thinking of reading alone 2nite. Maybe next time? RT **@Raven** Chillin' on this bust of Pallas Athena. Want 2 hang? #nevermore

———•·•———

@VirginiaWoolf Searching #craigslist for a cheap boat. #got2go2thelighthouse

———•·•———

@HermanMelville So nauseous. Can barely type. #seasick

———•·•———

@LeoTolstoy Some things never change. #warandpeace

———•·•———

@Homer There must be a fire on our block. #sirens

———•·•———

@FScottFitzgerald Have a hot date tonight—what should I bring her, tweeps? #tenderisthenight

@MarkTwain If you have nothing to say, say nothing. #twitterkiller

———•—•———

@LewisCarroll I'm late! #goaskalice

Artists

@AndyWarhol Already sold this Tweet for a cool million. #eatsoup

———•—•———

@JacksonPollock You know what else your kid can do?

———•—•———

@SalvadorDali Whoops! Just deleted an important file. Anyone know how 2 recover it? #persistenceofmemory

———•—•———

@ClaudeMonet What a terrible waste of time. #firstimpression

———•—•———

@MarkRothko Warm Tweet. #cooltweet

@FridaKahlo Funny. RT
@DiegoRivera Check out the
new Apple release! #iBrow

@MCEscher Plz stop tracing
my art. #tshirts4sale

@RichardAvedon OMG. I think
I've been shot. #selfportrait

@LeonardoDaVinci Have
to change the way I think
about things. #perspective

@Michelangelo Good idea. RT
@LeonardoDaVinci Have to
change the way I think about
things. #thelastjudgment

@AnselAdams The conditions in
my studio are really unbearable.
#bears

@PeterPaulRubens I'm going
to need a bigger canvas.

@VincentVanGogh What was that?

@PaulCezanne Nothing much
going on today. #stilllife

@EdvardMunch :-0

Historical Figures

@ChristopherColumbus Loving
yoga lately! #anewworld

@JesusChrist I, too, feel indecisive
sometimes . . . #wWjd

@AbrahamLincoln Remember
2 get out the vote 2morrow
and help the #Republicans
fight 4 equal rights! #LOL

@ThomasEdison Nice phone app, **@BenjaminFranklin**—too bad I INVENTED THE LIGHTBULB.

@AlbertEinstein Just bought a "smart" phone. #notimpressed

@NapoleonBonaparte Expanding my domain name. #worldwideweb

Meme's the Word

While Internet memes often feature an animal of some sort—from kittens to puppies to cockatoos—sometimes they can be cash cows, too. In 2005, a British student launched what he called The Million Dollar Homepage, which featured one million pixels that advertisers could purchase for one dollar a pixel. The site was quickly elevated to meme status and the site reached its goal in no more than five months.

@MahatmaGandhi Will b there.
RT **@PillowTalk** Flash civil
disobedience pillow fight—in food
court 2day at noon! #satyagraha

@SigmundFreud New Bluetooth
= dreamy. #oralphase

@MarcoPolo Polo.
RT **@PoolGuy** Marco.

@LouisXVI Losing it. #myhead

@SamuelMorse YHGTBK! #code

@CharlesDarwin I win.
#survivalofthefittest

@KingArthur Gwennie's being a
total drag today. Really rethinking
our relationship. #excalibur

@FranklinRoosevelt Give me five for three—or I walk. #newdeal

---

@GeorgeWashington I cannot tell a lie. #fingerscrossed

@IsaacNewton My calls keep getting dropped. #gravity #eyeroll

---

@AmeliaEarhart Need an iPhone GPS app—quick, what do my tweeples recommend? #lost

MILESTONES

When it's actually important

THE INCREASING POPULARITY
of smartphones has made it possible to share nearly every occasion.
Letting the world know how much
fun you're having is now manda-
tory. (Does a wedding even count
anymore if no one posts a picture
of the table settings?) Broadcast-
ing big events assures that your
momentous happenings receive the
attention they deserve.

What's the Password?

The Internet is still a pretty straightforward place thanks to the (often banal) reliability of human behavior. In the case of email passwords, for example, cracking the code is easier than it seems. A study done by the software company Imperva analyzed the passwords of 32 million people and found that the number one choice was "123456." Slightly less complicated was the second most popular password, "12345."

If social networks have taught us anything it's that we should celebrate every moment, regardless of how humdrum or noteworthy. Back in the day a newspaper announcement would broadcast big news (good or bad) but nowadays up-to-the-minute posts about life-changing events are expected.

In order to stand out from the

typical banal boast, it's important to leave no taboo or personal topic untapped as a possible posting resource. While assured crowd-pleasers include subjects covered in this chapter, don't be afraid to mine downright depressing (and sympathy-provoking) events and disasters. Misery loves company, but you can only fit the company of thousands into a room if it's a chat room.

The main point of social media is to be social, after all, and keeping friends and family abreast is ostensibly the purpose. At the very least, whatever the special occasion you're sure to save precious time by mass communication—and receive far more feedback and validation than a single phone call to dad could ever achieve.

Personal Tragedies

@Anonymous I can never stop at 140 characters. #ihaveaproblem

---

@ExGirlfriend She loves you not. RT **@ExBoyfriend** She loves me? #dramatictweets

---

@Fired At least I'll have some time to work on my pet project. #catpalace

---

@Spiritual Walking toward a bright light . . . #screensaver

@Divorced I'll be Tweeting from this account every other weekend. #sharedcustody

---

@FunDad Stocking up on soda and candy! RT **@PartyMom** At the store buying a cart of new video games! #custodybattle

@**GoodMourning** I swear it was just an accident. #droppedcall

---

@**Son** It's true, you really can never go back home again. #disowned

---

@**Fired** There's no one to blame but me. #selfemployed

@**Ex** I find that writing helps. #deaththreats

@**GoodMourning** Turning my ringer off. #momentofsilence

@**Sickbed** Don't know how long I'll last. #onebar

@**BrokenUp** It just didn't seem real until now. #statuschange

A Matter of Age

@Baby Here I am!
#bravenewworld

@Spouse Looking for a
new job. RT **@Retiree** Looking
forward to spending all day
every day with **@Spouse**!

@Midlife I've been deeply
affected by the current
recession. #hairline

@Senior Tweeting is such
a pain! #arthritis

@Retiree I've finally discovered
my passion in life! #sleepingin

@Midlife Reconnecting with the
younger generation. #trophywife

@**Senior** Rolling out of
here. Peace. #wheelchair

———•—•———

@**BirthdayWishes** I have a
heart condition. #surprise

———•—•———

@**Old** What hill? #overit

———•—•———

@**Senior** Headed to the restroom.
Constantly. #goldenyears

Tip: Mind UR Manners

Believe it or not, the names in your contact
list are real people with real feelings. While it
may be as easy as a click of a button to end a
"friendship," that doesn't mean you should do
it without considering online etiquette carefully. While it's okay (and far easier) to simply
ignore a friend request, if it comes from a
coworker or, worse, your boss, you don't have
much of a choice. Filters—both digital and
metaphorical—are your only options.

@Old Forgot what I was going to Tweet. #seniormoment

@Midlife Resting on my laurels is out of the question. #chronicbackpain

The Big Day

@Graduate1 Are we going to be graded on this ceremony? #fail

@Graduate2 I've never seen my parents cry like that. #movingbackhome

---

@Graduate3 I feel like the world owes me. #gratitude

@Graduate4 It's hard to put a value on the education that I've received at **@College**. #200K

@**BoyMitzvah** Looking for a Hebrew translator app. #torah4beginners

---

@**Anniversary** Can't believe we were married a year ago. Yesterday. #sorry

---

@**DeliveryDad** Money shot! #youtube

@**DeliveryMom** Don't you dare! That's not my good side. RT @**DeliveryDad** Money shot! #youtube

---

@**SweetSixteen** So frustrated and angry all the time. #driving

---

@**Anniversary** This year we're recreating our first date! #awkwardsex

---

@**Bride** Cue wedding march. #hereicome

The World Wide Web

The United States may be the birthplace of social networks, but even so, we're not as savvy—or popular—as we like to think. A report issued by The Nielsen Company states that 10 percent more Brazilians access blogs and social networks than Americans. That dedication seems to pay off—the BBC has reported that Brazilians maintain the second highest average number of online friends (231), topped only by Malaysians (233).

@**OvertheHill** 40 is soooo the new 20. #facelift

———•·•———

@**ReallyOvertheHill** And 60 is the new 40! #multipleprocedures RT @**OvertheHill** 40 is soooo the new 20. #facelift

———•·•———

@**BrisBabyDaddy** Feel faint. Stepping outside. #fortheloveofgod

Natural Disasters

@WatchTower Is it true that birds will fly away before an earthquake? Anyone? #notatweet

---

@NatureGirl GPS is broken. Don't know where I am. #backyard

@Homeowner Is it Christmas? Because I totally have a tree in my house. #hurricane

---

@Blonde Followed snowplow for 45 minutes before I realized he was plowing the parking lot. WTF?!?! #goingincircles

---

@ChickenLittle I had another dream last night—I mean it guys, this time I think it's really gonna happen. #thebigone

@Noah It's really coming down out there. #toldyouso

@VolcanoLover I met a really great girl this weekend! She could be the one! Super excited for tonight's date. #blowingit

---

@Survivor Doing my physical therapy. #fingerinjury

@HurricaneChaser Wind has died down. Finally getting reception again. Going outside to pick up a better signal. #eyeofthestorm

The Holidays

@Home4theHolidays Totally getting into the Christmas spirit. #eggnog

---

@Jolly Got knocked out by the punch. #christmascheer

@HolidayBeliever Just used some tinsel and string to fix my BlackBerry! It's a miracle! #34thtweet

———•·•———

@NewYears Will stop Tweeting everything about my life. #resolution

———•·•———

@NeighborhoodChoir Please RT: http://xmassong.mp3 #2cold2carol

———•·•———

@Scrooge I refuse to succumb to cheer pressure.

———•·•———

@Home4theHolidays Basking in the warm glow of the season. #watchingreruns

———•·•———

@XmasParty Standing under the mistletoe . . . #hinthint

@Grinch Freak storm just rolled in—won't be able to make it home this year. #:)

------•------

@XmasSpirit Low on funds but thought everyone would enjoy this animated .gif of a dancing cat wearing an elf hat with jinglebells! #goodwilltowardmemes

------•------

@Scrooge Holiday spirit is an oxymoron. #bahhumbug

------•------

@Home4theHolidays I just need a silent night. #frazzled

------•------

@Scrooge You knitted this all by yourself? #badgift

------•------

@XmasSpirit I just loved this so much, I knew you'd love it, too. #regift

@**Jolly** Strange, I mailed it
weeks ago. #forgotyourgift

—————◆—————

@**Home4theHolidays** Your holiday
décor is so . . . colorful! #giantinflatables

—————◆—————

@**NewYears** Let's ring in the
new year! #callmyphone

Facebook of Ages

Social networks might still be in their adoles-
cence, but there's no age cutoff for who logs
on. A Pew Internet study found that between
April 2009 and May 2010, the presence of
users aged 55-64 increased by 88 percent.
While the majority of Facebook users are still
between the ages of 18 to 34, in 2010, Twitter
followers mourned the death of Ivy Bean, a
104-year-old British woman who had held the
title of the world's oldest Tweeter.

FAMOUS
COMMUNIQUÉS

When the stars come out to update

MOST FAMOUS PEOPLE ARE NOT
only used to the spotlight—they
downright court it. What better
way to generate buzz and generally
indulge in self-indulgence than by
maintaining a strong online presence? From athletes to actors to
reality television stars, all eyes are
glued to the computer screen, and
the latest celebrity exploits provide
endless fodder.

Ghost Tweet

Staying famous means staying busy, and celebrities don't always have time to attend to mundane details—like Tweeting. To maintain an Internet presence, stars such as Britney Spears and 50 Cent have hired ghost Twitterers to post for them. Even Barack Obama, who harnessed social media during his presidential campaign and has tons of followers, let many of them down in 2009 when he revealed that he had never, personally, used Twitter.

Celebrities *are* infinitely fascinating, after all. They're beautiful, glamorous, crazy, and sometimes even talented. What's not to like? It's no surprise then that the web is practically overflowing with sightings, news, and gossip.

Regardless of whether they're rants or raves, celebrity posts also remind us of the thin line that separates us from them. Not only has social media granted us a peek behind the curtain, it's also beckoned quite a few to join the fray. In savvy hands, social networks can even be transformed into marketing machines that catapult *you* toward stardom.

While most celebrities wouldn't admit to checking out the competition, that doesn't mean they don't do it on the sly (in the form of an anonymous Internet search, of course). In this chapter you'll find a compilation of the most outrageous Tweets ever tweeted by public figures—in all their misspelled, ungrammatical, and uncensored glory. Brushing up on these famous communiqués will help ensure your updates are all A-list quality.

Physical Appearance

@Dolly_Parton I hope people realize that there is a brain underneath the hair and a heart underneath the boobs.

@LisaRinna wow you look so much better in person . . . #offensivecompliments

---

@ElizabethBanks When I have a big zit on my face, I cheer myself up by telling myself "you look like a teenager!" It works 14% of the time.

@RainnWilson When Im 60 I want to look like Meryl Streep. And I mean EXACTLY like Meryl Streep.

@Oprah (Oprah Winfrey) no i'm not wearing a weave

@JohnCMayer I need to get back into the gym. I'm all for having boobs against my chest but not when they're mine.

————•+•————

@BobSaget Got a pedicure today. Liked it til the lady tried to give me a happy ending.

————•+•————

@BetteMidler It didn't used to be like this. Years ago, stars had glamour . . . and pubic hair.

————•+•————

@Cher Beauty Is not EVEN Skin Deep

————•+•————

@NickyHilton I take it personal when people call my cats fat :/

————•+•————

@WilliamShatner I've been told my damaged star on the Canadian Walk of Fame has been fixed. I wish I could replace my face as easily. My best, Bill

Mundane Details

@ParisHilton Yesterday was fun! I love the color pink :) -

———•———

@TheLittleIdiot (Moby) i just saw a juvenile coyote wandering around in front of my house. he looked lost. poor little coyote. i hope he finds his friends soon.

———•———

@JoshGroban I get freaked out shopping in rug stores. I mean, just stacks and stacks of rugs. Piled 4 feet high sometimes! Rolled against the walls!

———•———

@AshleyTisdale My tummy hurts today :(

———•———

@NeilDiamond My dog Poker is very reasonable. I like that.

@**ThatKevinSmith** On the Idaho/
Montana border, we see a herd of
buffalo, roaming. I find no desire for a
home, but could do with a
@**Chickfila** #LiveNudeSMod

@**KanyeWest** I specifically
ordered persian rugs with cherub
imagery!!! What do I have to do
to get a simple persian rug with
cherub imagery uuuuugh

Follow the Leaders

Hopeful politicians might consider spending
less time kissing babies and more time
online. During the 2010 midterm election, the
Facebook blog noted that in 74 percent of
races for the House and 81 percent of those
for the Senate, the winning candidate boasted
more Facebook fans. Meanwhile, Election Day
Twitter feeds were used to accurately forecast
the outcome of the Nevada Senate race while
traditional polls generally failed to do so.

@HankAzaria I like deviled eggs, but not enough to eat them.

@ChrisCornell I had shrimp last night again. Thought you should know. Ryan Gosling is a good actor. Peace out

Gossip and Rebuttals

@PerezHilton @SpencerPratt Are you smoking your sister's meth?

@ConanOBrien @LanceArmstrong —I was drunk. And I wanted some tips for smoother legs. Is that so wrong?

@KirstieAlley Don't worry about Dave Letterman making snide remarks about me, my sweet fans . . . He's just grumpy since he had to quit banging his interns.

@JimGaffigan The Hummer limo is really the douche bag chariot.

@DiabloCody I love people that go to gossip sites and type "WHO CARES?" in the comments. You do, you little cutie!

@Joan_Rivers Life's VERY different since shooting my documentary. Cameras no longer follow me around. Now I know what it feels like to be Sharon Stone.

@CourtneyLoveUK But then again I dont pick fights with insanely deluded irrevelant friendless unatractive children who noone i know even close to likes.

@CraigyFerg (Craig Ferguson) Today I've had my teeth scraped by a dentist and been scolded by twattybugs who thought I was tweeting & driving. #betterthanbeingmelgibson

Popularity Contest

Not surprisingly for a phenomenon based upon social connections—and ostensibly, popularity—social media itself has become one of the most in-demand Internet destinations. Email, long the definitive means of online communication, was surpassed in 2008 in terms of usage by social networking, according to The Nielsen Company. The new media is so entrenched that it has even knocked porn from its reign as the most searched for topic.

@SandraBernhard what is the turning point when two famous people who are dating throw in the towel? do they run out of conversation & stare into the mirror?

Self-Promotion

@MichaelIanBlack He died as he lived, trying to popularize hashtag games. #onmytombstone

@NicoleRichie T.G.I.F. Thank God I'm Flamboyant.

***

@RiversCuomo As usual, I'm like a hundred times cooler than everyone else.

***

@BoyGeorge I used to go back for more cabbage at school, I'm weird!

***

@The_Real_Shaq (Shaquille O'Neal) #thereshouldbealaw against bein dis good lookin

***

@IAmDiddy (Sean Combs) Taken a bubble bath holdin a oscar!! God is great Let's go people

***

@RealTracyMorgan The wait is over! The black Svengali has arrived! I'm on the street turning good girls bad and getting them pregnant!!!

@StephenatHome (Stephen Colbert) See you at the emmys this weekend! To help you recognize me, i'll be the one holding an emmy.

------•·•------

@SpencerPratt The new book will be equal parts Tolstoy & Hemingway. Maybe less Tolstoy than Hemingway.

------•·•------

@SnoopDogg who saw me on Jeopardy?

------•·•------

@Vincent_Gallo THIS IS A PROMISE! If you find me and have maple syrup we can take a photo together. Also; I will sign your maple syrup.

Overshare

@Danny_DeVito Great movie. IMAX in Burbank. Smaller screen but great picture. Like to bang one of those ten foot broads!

@JessicaSimpson On my way to workout with my trainer. everytime we have to do squats and he yells at me 'get lower like you're in the club.' I don't squat in the club unless I'm peeing.

@AndyDick Intervention #11 last week was a real party! Thanks friends and family. Love you!

@TyraBanks Sometimes, the taste in my mouth from the meal I just ate still is yummy. Makes me delay teeth brushing for one hour.

@JoseCanseco I am on the toilet thinking about writing a third book

@JayMohr37 whenever I want the hotel jacuzzi to myself, I sit facing the jets. No one bothers me when I do that.

@DaveNavarro6767 When I look at going to the dentist as a kind of BDSM appointment, it really isn't all that bad.

--·--

@LaurenConrad Just watched a dude take his earings out of his ears and put them in his nipples . . . While standing on a street corner. Gotta love LA.

--·--

@HeidiMontag Giving myself a soft tissue breast massage. Ladies we have to keep those breast implants soft.

--·--

@MileyCyrus Good morning everyone. Life is good. I am lying in bed with my mommy right now scratching her bug bites.

Celeb Wisdom

@AlyssaMilano There are two types of people in this world. People who think farts are funny and people that don't.

@DameElizabeth (Elizabeth Taylor)
Life without earrings is empty!

━━━━•◦•━━━━

@APlusk (Ashton Kutcher) When
life blows sometimes the best
thing you can be is a dick.

━━━━•◦•━━━━

@JimmyKimmel lubricant?
I say lubriCAN!

WWJT?

Technology is like a religion to some people—
and religious leaders are starting to catch
on. The Dalai Lama's Twitter feed, for instance,
sends near-daily words of wisdom along
with updates on public appearances to his
million-plus followers. The Vatican has also
transcended the digital divide, offering an
application to post a virtual postcard of the
Pope to friends' Facebook walls as well as a
YouTube channel.

@YokoOno Imagine 1000 suns in the sky @ same time. Let them shine for Ihr. Then let them gradually melt into the sky. Make 1 tunafish sandwich & eat.

@RustyRockets (Russell Brand) The Orion Nebula viewed from Earth makes Human conflict seem a bit silly. We're all one rock, we might as well attack our own feet.

@EbertChicago (Roger Ebert) Cleavage. It speaks to us from the time before memory of love, comfort, warmth, softness and food. Cleavage. Oh yes. Cleavage.

@CarrieFFisher We're always fighting numbers: Time, (deadines, age) money, (bills, prices, salaries) temperature (fever, altitudes) weight (too fat,too thin)

@RedHourBen (Ben Stiller) Turtles are amazing. Really.

@**MarthaStewart** Bons mots d'aujourdhui: take the eggs on vacation not the chickens

———•••———

@**JeremyPiven** The sun doesn't ask the earth for a thanks for shining on it . . . We do our jobs and that my friends has to be it!

———•••———

@**TomWaits** If there's one thing you can say about mankind, there's nothing kind about man.

———•••———

@**SteveMartinToGo** Did you know it's possible to Tweet a concise, grammatical, correctly punctuated sentence that is exactly one hundred forty characters long?

@Procreator Anything for a free phone.
#familyplan